Child Care Law: Scotland
A summary

Alexandra Plumtree

British Agencies for Adoption and Fostering

Contents

Abbreviations

AALL(S)R 1996
Adoption Allowance (Scotland) Regulations 1996

AA(S)R 1996
Adoption Agencies (Scotland) Regulations 1996

ALA(S)R 1996
Arrangements to Look After Children (Scotland) Regulations 1996

ALC(S)A 1991
Age of Legal Capacity (Scotland) Act 1991

A(S)A 1978
Adoption (Scotland) Act 1978

AS(CC etc) 1997
Act of Sederunt (Child Care and Maintenance Rules) 1997*

CA 1975
Children Act 1975

CA 1989
Children Act 1989

CH(S)R 1996
Children's Hearings (Scotland) Rules 1996

CP(S)A 1995
Criminal Procedure (Scotland) Act 1995

CSA 1991
Child Support Act 1991

C(S)A 1995
Children (Scotland) Act 1995

CYP(S)A 1937
Children and Young Persons (Scotland) Act 1937

FC(PF)(S) R 1985
Foster Children (Private Fostering) (Scotland) Regulations 1985

FC(S)A 1984
Foster Children (Scotland) Act 1984

FC(S)R 1996
Fostering of Children (Scotland) Regulations 1996

FLA
Family Law Act 1986

SW(S)A 1968
Social Work (Scotland) Act 1968

*Rules of Court for Sheriff Court applications for Adoption, Parental Responsibilities Orders (PROs), Child Assessment Orders (CAOs), Child Protection Orders (CPOs), Exclusion Orders (EOs) and children's hearing cases

Foreword

This book summarises child care law in Scotland and takes account of all the changes introduced by the Children (Scotland) Act 1995. It simplifies the complex language of law without losing the necessary precision that the law requires.

It will be particularly useful to those whose professional or personal circumstances require them to be aware of the law relating to children and families. As well as providing a short description of child care law it also identifies where, in the various statutes, the detail of the law can be found.

This book makes a very helpful contribution to enhancing our knowledge of child care law in Scotland.

Peter Cassidy
Director of Social Work, Aberdeen Council, and Chair of the Scotland Committee of BAAF

Preface

This booklet is the fourth and substantially revised edition of BAAF's existing title, *Child Care Law: A summary of the law in Scotland.* It takes account of the great changes since the previous volume by MacLeod and Giltinan (1992) and particularly the provisions of the Children (Scotland) Act 1995 and its supporting Regulations, Rules and Rules of Court.

As with previous editions, this book is not a detailed legal textbook about what is a wide-reaching area of law. Rather, it aims to provide a basic framework of the law for those who do not need to know more and a starting point for those who have to look further. Statutory references are given throughout the text, there is a glossary of terms and a brief list of further reading.

I should like to thank all of those who have given and continue to give me the benefit of their views on the many issues of law and practice that are continuously arising in this area of law. In particular, however, I am grateful to Professor Kathleen Marshall of the Centre for the Study of the Child & Society at the University of Glasgow, for reading the text in draft and providing detailed comments and corrections. Any mistakes remaining are, of course, mine.

I am also grateful to all my colleagues in the BAAF Scottish Centre for their help and support, and to Miranda Davies and Shaila Shah in our Publications Department in London.

Alexandra Plumtree LLB

The law is stated as at 1 September 1997.

Note about the author

Alexandra Plumtree is a solicitor and the Scottish Legal Consultant for BAAF. She has worked in private practice and as a reporter to the children's panel, and has extensive experience of the public and private law of the family and children in Scotland, including the Children (Scotland) Act 1995.

1

Principles and themes

This chapter deals with general themes and principles in the law of Scotland relating to children, some but not all of which were introduced by the Children (Scotland) Act 1995.

Definition of 'child'

1.1

There is no one definition of child in the law of Scotland. Whether a young person is a 'child' or not will depend on the particular legislation and/or circumstances. However, as a rule of thumb, 16-year-olds in Scotland can do most things legally except vote, buy alcohol and have a homosexual relationship (18) or drive (17). In private disputes between parents the law usually regulates the position only up to 16, although parents are obliged to pay maintenance for their children beyond that time and until they finish all education. Where a child is looked after by the local authority, that care can last up to 18.

Some other definitions

1.2

There is a distinction between criminal and civil law. Criminal law is self-explanatory and, for the purposes of this book, anything which is not criminal will be treated as civil.

1.3

Another distinction is made between private and public law. For the purposes of this book, private law relates to matters between private individuals and their rights and responsibilities in relation to each other. Public law deals with the ways in which society and the state become involved in the lives of children and families. Adoption law straddles this divide, as it is a private law action in the courts, but often (not always) comes about because of public law intervention by the local authority.

Overarching principles

1.4

The Children (Scotland) Act 1995 sets out three overarching principles which apply to most decisions in the areas of the law that the Act deals with. Those areas are private law, local authority duties, child protection measures, the children's hearing system, Parental Responsibilities Orders and adoption. The three principles are:

Child's welfare to be paramount consideration

1.5

This is not completely new in all cases but is the test which now applies in court decisions, children's hearing decisions and local authority and adoption agencies' decisions about welfare in the areas listed above. In private law cases this has been the test since 1986, but in adoption matters the test was previously 'first consideration' of the child's welfare. In fact, the adoption test is that the child's welfare throughout the child's life shall be of paramount consideration.

C(S)A 1995, s. 11(7)(a), s. 16(1), s. 17(1)(a) & A(S)A 1978, s. 6(1)(a)

Consideration of the child's views

1.6

Courts, children's hearings, local authorities and adoption agencies all have a duty to allow children to express their views about their situations, and to take account of these views in their decisions. While this has been good practice in many areas, it is now formally specified as a duty in these situations. There is no *lower* age limit. The Act says that any child who is 12 or over is presumed to have a view, but this implies that a younger child can have a view although he or she is not presumed to have one. It is necessary to find out if the child has a view, whether he or she wishes to express it, and then take account of it. This does not mean the same thing as doing exactly what the child wants.

C(S)A 1995 s. 6(1), s. 11(7)(b) & (10), s. 16(2) & (4), s. 17(3) & (4) & s. 25(5) & A(S)A 1978 s. 6(1)(b)(i) & (2)

No order

1.7

This principle is sometimes called the 'minimum necessary intervention' principle. It states that no court order or children's hearing requirement shall be made unless the court/hearing thinks that making an order is better for the child than not making it. This does *not* mean that making an order is a 'last resort'. It means that the court or hearing must be certain that an order is necessary for the child's welfare, and that the order they are making is the best one. If the child's welfare can be secured as paramount consideration without an order or with less of an order, that is what should be done. Adoption agencies have a similar duty when they are making any decisions relating to the adoption/freeing of a child: they must consider alternatives.

C(S)A s. 11(7)(a) & s. 16 (3) & (4); A(S)A 1978 s. 6A & s. 24 (3)

Consideration of religious persuasion, racial, cultural and linguistic heritage

1.8

This principle was introduced by the 1995 Act but does not apply to all areas of law. It applies to decisions that the local authority make in relation to children whom they are 'looking after' or whom they are treating as 'in need'. It is also a duty on adoption agencies and courts in any decision relating to adoption. There is also case law indicating that these matters are important and need to be considered in private law cases (Osborne *v* Matthan, 18 October 1996, reported 1997 SLT 811).

C(S)A 1995, s. 17(4)(c) & s. 22(2); A(S)A 1978 s. 6(1)(b)(ii)

Capacity of children: criminal and civil

1.9

The age of criminal capacity in Scotland is eight.

1.10

The age of civil capacity in Scotland is generally 16, but with specific exceptions. These are that the child:

- May carry out normal transactions (eg. buy sweets, trainers, etc);
- May make a will if 12 or over;
- Must be asked if he or she consents to adoption if 12 or over (unless incapable);
- Must be the person to consent or otherwise to medical, dental and surgical treatment if, in the opinion of the qualified medical practitioner, he or she is capable of understanding the nature and possible consequences of the treatment;
- May instruct a solicitor in any civil matter if he or she has a general understanding of what it means to do so.

ALC(S)A 1991 s. 1 & s. 2

1.11

The most striking of these points are the rights to consent to medical treatment and to instruct a solicitor.

Working co-operatively

1.12

Good co-operative working between all individuals making decisions about children or working with them is positively encouraged by the 1995 Act. There is an expectation that parents will work together and with their children in all decisions about welfare, even if the parents themselves do not get on. There is an expectation that, where the local authority is involved with children and families, they will work co-operatively and in partnership with them.

Local authority

1.13

'Local authority' is defined in the 1995 Act as meaning the whole local authority and all its departments, not just the social work department. This is a change from the position under the Social Work (Scotland) Act 1968. It means that the whole local authority are obliged to carry out responsibilities, duties, etc. when they are owed to children and families, whether the children are 'in need', 'looked after' or requiring other services.

C(S)A 1995 s. 93(1)

Medical consent for children

1.14

For information about this see the above para 1.10.

2

The criminal system and Scottish courts

This chapter outlines briefly some points about the Scottish criminal system in general and explains the Scottish court structure. Different decisions are made in different courts. Who makes a decision and the procedure used depends on which court is dealing with a case.

The Scottish criminal system

2.1

In Scotland, the adult criminal system is not used for most cases involving crimes alleged to have been committed by children under 16. Even though the age of criminal capacity is eight, most children are not prosecuted in the courts. Instead they are referred by the police to the reporter to the children's panel, who decides whether to take the case to a hearing (see Chapter 8). The exception to this rule is where a child is charged with a more serious offence, such as a severe assault or murder. In those circumstances the child will be dealt with by the adult criminal system.

2.2

By and large, the police report children under 16 only to the reporter. They may also report cases to the Procurator Fiscal, who represents locally the independent Scottish prosecution service. If a case is jointly reported, the Procurator Fiscal makes the ultimate decision about whether the child is dealt with as an adult or a child. Even over 16, a child need not be dealt with in the adult system if he or she is still subject to a supervision requirement in the hearing system.

2.3

If a child is prosecuted, the decision, as for adults, is made by the prosecution service (headed by the Crown Office) on the basis of the following questions:

- Is there sufficient evidence? and
- Is it in the public interest to prosecute?

The prosecution decides what offence a person will be charged with and which court will deal with the matter. A case is either summary, when it is dealt with by a judge alone, or solemn, when it is dealt with by a judge and jury. If a child is prosecuted, it will often be a serious case and therefore a judge and jury will hear it.

The court system

2.4

The Scottish court system is reasonably straightforward: three courts deal with criminal and three deal with civil matters. As will be seen, the Sheriff Court operates in both types of cases and deals with the widest variety of matters. Scotland is divided into six Sheriffdoms and each Sheriffdom has a Sheriff Principal. There are fifty Sheriff Court Districts, each of which has a court where a Sheriff sits regularly. Sheriffs are either permanent judges, or temporary part-time judges. Both of these have to be legally qualified and have had a number of years' experience. Honorary Sheriffs are appointed locally to deal with certain matters when there is a shortage of other Sheriffs. They are usually not legally qualified and have very limited powers.

2.5

Sheriffs Principal and Sheriffs are addressed as 'My lord' or 'My lady' in court and 'Sheriff' when off the bench.

Criminal courts

The District Court

2.6

This court deals only with minor criminal matters. Cases are dealt with by one or more lay unqualified justices, sitting with a legally qualified clerk. As in all criminal courts, cases come to this one on the basis of a decision by the prosecution service.

The Sheriff Court

2.7

The Sheriff Court deals with the bulk of criminal cases in Scotland. It deals both with summary matters (lesser crimes) where the Sheriff sits and hears the case on his or her own and more serious cases, heard by the Sheriff sitting with a jury. Again, the decision to take a case to the Sheriff Court, and which type of case it is to be, is made by the prosecution service.

The High Court of Justiciary

2.8

This is the court which deals with very serious criminal trials and with all criminal appeals in Scotland. The judges are legally qualified senior High Court judges, addressed as 'My lord' or 'My lady'.

2.9

If the court is dealing with a criminal trial, this is done by a single judge sitting with a jury. The court can try all crimes, but usually only deals with very serious ones. Only the High Court can deal with murder, treason and rape. The court goes on circuit round the country.

2.10

When the court is sitting to hear appeals, it sits only in Edinburgh. A group of three or more judges will hear criminal appeals, from the District Court and the Sheriff Court, as well as from High Court trials. This is the final Court of Appeal in Scotland for criminal matters. There is no criminal appeal in Scotland to the House of Lords.

Civil courts

The Sheriff Court

2.11

The Sheriff Court deals with a wide variety of civil matters. Only the Sheriff Court can deal with children's hearing proof cases, appeals from children's hearings and applications about Parental Responsibilities Orders. The Sheriff Court deals with many cases of divorce and disputes about children and adoption, although these can also be raised in the Court of Session.

2.12

An appeal from the Sheriff can go either to the Sheriff Principal for that area or straight to the Court of Session. If there is an appeal to the Sheriff Principal, there may be a further appeal on to the Court of Session. Where a case is raised, and where the appeal goes, are decisions for the person raising the case and the person who appeals.

The Court of Session

2.13

This court deals with civil cases from the beginning, and also appeals in civil cases from the Sheriff and/or Sheriff Principal. It sits only in Edinburgh. The judges are the same as those who sit in the High Court of Justiciary.

If a case is started in the Court of Session, it is heard by a single judge in the 'Outer House'. If the court is sitting as an appeal court, a group of three or more judges sits to hear the case in the 'Inner House'. They deal with appeals from the Sheriff Court, the Sheriffs Principal and the Outer House.

The senior judge in Scotland and the head of the Scottish legal system is the Lord President of the Court of Session. He is also the Lord Justice General in criminal cases.

House of Lords

2.14

There is an appeal in some but not all civil matters from the Court of Session to the House of Lords. Adoption appeals and appeals in disputes about children go to the House of Lords, but appeals in children's hearing cases cannot do so.

Cases are heard by an appellate (appeal) committee of the House of Lords. The judges are called Lords of Appeal in Ordinary or Law Lords. Usually five of them hear a case and if it is Scottish two of those judges will, by convention, be Scottish. At any one time, there are always two Scottish Law Lords.

These judges sit in the House of Lords as Life Peers, the senior Law Lord being the Lord Chancellor. He is also speaker of the House of Lords, and is a political appointment. He is head of the legal system for England and Wales, but *not* of the Scottish legal system.

3

Parental responsibilities and rights – private law

This chapter deals with parental responsibilities and rights in relation to children. It covers who has them, who can get them and how, together with how the court deals with disputes in this area.

Parental responsibilities and rights

3.1

The 1995 Act introduced the terminology of 'parental responsibilities and rights', instead of just 'parental rights'. Traditionally, Scots Law treated children as the possession of their parents but the 1995 Act moves away from this, towards treating children as people who do have their own rights as well.

3.2

Sections 1 and 2 of the 1995 Act deal with responsibilities and rights, and make it clear that no one can have rights unless they have responsibilities first. The responsibilities are to safeguard and protect the child's welfare, to provide guidance, to maintain contact if not living with the child and to act as the child's legal representative if need be. The rights are the right to have the child living with him or her, to control, direct or guide the child, to maintain contact and the right to act as the child's legal representative if need be.

C(S)A 1995 s. 1 & s. 2

3.3

These rights and responsibilities can be exercised individually by any person having them, without having to obtain the consent of anyone else who also has them. The only exception is that the child cannot be removed from the United Kingdom without the consent of every person who has the responsibilities and rights of residence and/or contact *and* is exercising them.

C(S)A 1995 s. 2(2), (3) & (6)

3.4

All genetic parents are obliged to maintain a child even if they do not have any reponsibilities unless the child has been adopted or made the subject of an order under the Human Fertilisation and Embryology Act 1990. This is not directly dealt with by the 1995 Act. Since the coming into force of the Child Support Act 1991, where parents have separated and there is a dispute about maintenance, the Child Support Agency will usually be involved and there are few court disputes about these matters.

CSA 1991

Who has responsibilities and rights automatically?

3.5

The mother of a child always has parental responsibilities and rights unless and until these are taken away from her by some form of court process such as adoption.

3.6

A father only has parental responsibilities and rights if he has been or is married to the mother at the time of the child's conception or anytime subsequently. Where a couple are married and have children, both parents will have responsibilities and rights. If the couple are not married, the father does not have those responsibilities and rights automatically. If he marries the mother at *any* time after the child's birth, he acquires these. If a man marries a woman with children, but he is not the genetic father, he does not acquire parental responsibilities and rights because of the marriage.

C(S)A 1995 s. 3

The rights of unmarried fathers

3.7

An unmarried genetic or birth father can acquire parental responsibilities and rights by using the agreement provided for in the 1995 Act. There is a very straightforward form provided, which, if it is is signed by both genetic parents and sent for registration to the Books of Council and Session (a public register), gives the father parental responsibilities and rights as if he had married the mother. There is a small cost for this, but no formal procedure is involved, and there is no need to go to court. Forms are available from organisations such as Citizens Advice Bureaux.

C(S)A 1995 s. 4

3.8

This form provides a straightforward way for couples to give the unmarried father responsibilities without going to court or being involved in a dispute. There is no need for the couple to live together. Once this agreement is signed and registered, the couple cannot change their minds. The only way to alter the arrangements after that is to go to court.

3.9

An unmarried father can also use the court to get parental responsibilities and rights. He will have to do this if the mother disagrees with his request for responsibilities and rights, and refuses to sign the form. An unmarried father may also want to use the court if he does not want all responsibilities and rights but only, say, contact. Applications of this type go to court in terms of section 11 of the 1995 Act (see paras 3.10–18).

C(S)A 1995 s. 11

Section 11 applications and orders

3.10

This section allows courts (the Sheriff Court or Court of Session) to make any type of order about parental responsibilities and rights, guardianship or a child's property. The court can make an order because it has been asked to do so, or simply because, in any other case, it thinks an order is necessary.

C(S)A 1995 s. 11(1), (2) & (3)

3.11

The most common types of orders are:
- Residence orders;
- Contact orders;
- Specific issue orders;
- Interdicts;
- Orders taking away some or all of a person's parental responsibilities and rights.

C(S)A 1995 s. 11(2)

3.12

Any person can use this section, provided they can show an interest in the child. This includes all parents with responsibilities and rights, birth fathers without such responsibilities and anyone else claiming to have an interest. The only individuals who cannot use the court in this way are people who have already lost their parental responsibilities and rights because of adoption, freeing orders or Parental Responsibilities Orders.

C(S)A 1995 s. 11(3) & (4)

3.13

The local authority cannot use this section, but children can use it, as well as adults.

C(S)A 1995 s. 11(5)

3.14

The overarching principles (see Chapter 1) apply to all decisions made by the court under this section.

C(S)A 1995 s.11(7) & (10)

3.15

The previous law relating to children talked about 'custody'. The replacement term for custody is now 'residence' although it does *not* mean the same thing. A residence order may be granted to a parent who has parental responsibilities already, or it may be granted to someone who does not have any parental responsibilities to begin with, such as a grandparent or unmarried father.

3.16

If a residence order is granted to a parent with responsibilities and rights, in a divorce action or the like, the order simply states where the child is to live. It does not take away the non-residential parent's responsibilities and rights, apart from residence, and it encourages parents to work together for their children. This means that the two parents with parental responsibilities will be expected to continue to carry these out, even if they are separated or divorced. They both still have rights too.

3.17

If a residence order is granted to a person who does not already have responsibilities and rights, the order allows that person to have all the parental responsibilities and rights that are needed to care properly for the child. It does not, however, take responsibilities and rights away from anyone else who already has them, unless the court specifically orders that.

C(S)A 1995 s. 11(12)

3.18

Because the principle of minimum necessary intervention applies in these decisions, courts should no longer grant orders to disputing parents just because parents want them. The court will have to be satisfied, taking the child's welfare as paramount, that the order wanted is necessary for the child and that it is better to make the order than not to do so. Again, this represents a move away from giving a lump of custodial rights to one parent in a dispute and leaving the other parent with a feeling of very little involvement.

Interdicts and enforcement

3.19

As has already been mentioned, section 11 orders can include interdicts about children, including an interdict to prevent a child being removed from someone's care, if this is necessary to protect the child.

C(S)A 1995 s. 11(2)(f)

3.20

Orders made in Scotland in relation to children are recognised and may be enforced in other parts of the United Kingdom. Orders made elsewhere in the United Kingdom are also recognised and can be enforced in Scotland.

FLA 1986

Children 'looked after' by the local authority

3.21

The responsibilities of the local authority in this area are dealt with in Chapter 7.

3.22

However, there is a question about parents' rights when a child is 'looked after' by a local authority, either on a voluntary basis or because of a supervision requirement from the children's hearing system.

3.23

If a child is accommodated by the local authority, this is a voluntary arrangement with the consent of the parents and they do not lose parental responsibilities and rights. If they have any dispute with the local authority, they can ask for the child to be returned to them.

C(S)A 1995 s. 25

3.24

If a child is subject to a supervision requirement in the hearing system, the child may be at home or away from home. If the child is at home, the parental responsibilities and rights are only interfered with to the extent that the local authority has a responsibility to supervise.

3.25

However, if a child is away from home on a supervision requirement the parents' responsibilities and rights will be interfered with to some extent. They cannot demand return of the child. If there is a requirement, the courts cannot use section 11 to make orders about contact; only the children's hearing system can do this.

3.26

If someone wants to use section 11 to obtain a residence order for a child on a supervision requirement away from home, the court may grant such an order but the supervision requirement still takes precedence. If the court grants an order to the carer named by the hearing system (eg. a grandparent) then there is no conflict. If an order is granted to someone with whom the child does not live, it cannot be enforced unless and until the supervision requirement is terminated or varied to name that person.

Section 54 referrals

3.27

This section of the 1995 Act allows any civil court in a wide range of cases, including adoption, to refer a child to the reporter to the children's panel. The Sheriff finds grounds for referral established, and asks the reporter to consider the case. It is up to the reporter to decide whether to refer the child to a hearing. This is now the way in which a court dealing with private law cases refers a child into the public law system if the court is concerned about the arrangements for the child (see Chapter 8 on the hearing system).

C(S)A 1995 s. 54

3.28

The courts no longer have powers to place a child directly into the care of the local authority or under supervision in private law cases.

C(S)A 1995 Schedule 5

4

Private arrangements

This chapter deals with private care arrangements which parents and families may make for their children at home, with relatives or with other people.

At home and with family

4.1

If parents make arrangements for the care of their children at home by someone like an au pair, there are no controls over these although they could be liable criminally if the arrangements are inadequate.

CYP(S)A 1937 s. 12

4.2

Similarly, if a parent makes arrangements for a child to be cared for by a relative away from home, there is no statutory control or involvement.

4.3

Obviously, babysitting arrangements are included in this. Babysitters, like any other carer of a child without parental responsibilities, have a general duty to safeguard the child's welfare. They may also be able to consent to medical treatment in certain circumstances, provided they are at least 16 and *if* the child is too young to consent and they have no reason to believe the parent would refuse to do so.

C(S)A 1995 s. 5

4.4

It is not an offence to leave children under 16 unattended, but if harm or neglect is suffered by the children, the person who left them unattended may be charged with a criminal offence. This applies to parents and any other carers who are 16 or over.

CYP(S)A 1937 s. 12

Childminding

4.5

A childminder is someone who:
a) looks after one or more children under eight in a private house for payment for more than two hours in any day; and
b) is not a parent, relative or foster carer of the child and does not have parental responsibilities.

CA 1989 s. 71(2) & (4)

4.6

A nanny is not a childminder if she or he is looking after a child in the home of her or his employer.

CA 1989 s. 71(5)

4.7

A childminder must register with the local authority. There are conditions for registration and it may be refused. In addition, the local authority must make inspections of the childminder's home and arrangements. There is an annual inspection fee as a condition of continued registration.

CA 1989 ss. 71–4, s. 76 & s. 77

4.8

If a childminder is unregistered, he or she may be served with an enforcement notice and breach of this is a criminal offence.

CA 1989 s. 78

Nurseries and day care

4.9

The local authority have a duty to provide day care for certain children 'in need' (see Chapter 5).

C(S)A 1995 s. 27

4.10

However, in terms of the general provision of day care, local authorities must keep a register of people who provide it. This register covers the provision of day care for children under eight on premises other than private houses and for a period of more than two hours every day. Such day care may be used by the local authority because of their duties under the 1995 Act or it may be used in private arrangements by families.

4.11

In both circumstances, however, the registration must be done by the local authority which impose certain conditions. These include specifying the number of children able to be cared for and the number of helpers. Registration may be refused or cancelled and it is an offence for an unregistered person to provide day care.

CA 1989 s. 71, s. 73, s. 74, s. 76 & s. 77

<

Private fostering

4.12

This type of foster care is provided on a private basis by arrangement between parents and a non-relative. It is to be distinguished from foster care arranged by the local authority, where the local authority make such arrangements and place a child with approved foster carers. Such public fostering makes a child a 'looked after' child and is dealt with in Chapter 7.

4.13

Separate legislation covers private fostering arrangements. For these arrangements a foster child is one who is under compulsory school leaving age and is cared for by someone who is not a relative or guardian. Further, the care must be for more than 28 days.

FC(S)A 1984 s. 1 & s. 2

4.14

Where such private arrangements are made, the parent and foster carer must notify the local authority not less than two weeks before the arrangement starts, unless it is an emergency. In the case of an emergency, notification must be made within one week.

FC(S)A 1984, s. 4 & s. 5; FC (PF)(S)R 1985

4.15

When the local authority are notified, they have a duty to be satisfied about the well-being of the child. The child must be visited within one week of the placement and on a regular basis thereafter. The authority may prohibit such a private arrangement, or impose conditions on the arrangement if they are not satisfied.

FC(S)A 1984 s. 3, s. 9 & s. 10 and FC(PF)(S)AR 1985

4.16

Some people may be disqualified from being private foster carers, including those convicted of certain criminal offences and/or those who have been refused registration or removed from registration as childminders.

FC(S)A 1984 s. 7

4.17

Private foster carers who are caring for children do not have parental responsibilities and rights. They have general rights of control because they are acting in the place of parents. They must usually return the child to his or her parents on request unless they have obtained some other court authority to keep the child.

4.18

Private foster carers have a general obligation to safeguard and protect the child's welfare and the right to consent to medical treatment in certain circumstances, as mentioned in para 4.3 above.

C(S)A 1995 s. 5

5

General local authority duties to children

This chapter deals with the general duties of local authorities to all children in their area, and in particular towards children 'in need'. These provisions are concerned with what is generally seen as preventive work.

General welfare duty

5.1

Local authorities continue to be under a statutory duty to promote social welfare generally for all people in their area, by giving advice, guidance and assistance. Under these provisions, they may give assistance in kind to children and families, and in cash and kind to those over 18.

SW(S)A 1968 s. 12 as amended by C(S)A 1995 Schedule 4 para 15(11)

Children 'in need'

5.2

The 1995 Act introduced a definition of children 'in need' as being children for whom as wide a range as possible of services should be provided, to promote their welfare and to assist them to develop. The main provision is in section 22 of the 1995 Act, but it does not simply replace the above mentioned general duty to do preventive work.

C(S)A 1995 s. 22

5.3

In practice, local authorities use their powers under section 22 to provide services to children 'in need', and may also use section 12 of the 1968 Act as well.

5.4

The duty to provide services to children 'in need' allows local authorities, as long as they consider a child to be 'in need', to provide services for him or her, for his or her family if they safeguard the child's welfare and/or for any other member of the family, if they help the child. These services may be in cash or kind.

C(S)A 1995 s. 22 (3)

5.5

The definition of 'in need' is very wide, and each local authority require to have instructions and guidance so that individual decisions can be made about children and families. A child will be considered 'in need' if he or she is:

- Unlikely to achieve or maintain or have the opportunity of achieving or maintaining a reasonable standard of health or development unless he or she receives services; or
- His or her health or development is likely significantly to be impaired or further impaired unless services are provided; or
- He or she is disabled; or
- He or she is adversely affected by the disability of any other person in the family.

C(S)A 1995 s. 93(4)(a)

5.6

Disability is defined as 'chronically sick or disabled or [suffering] from mental disorder (within the meaning of the Mental Health (Scotland) Act 1984)'.

C(S)A 1995 s. 23(2)

5.7

If a child is 'in need' because of disability, the local authority have added duties to carry out an assessment of the child or any other disabled person in the family, to determine his or her needs. They must also assess the ability of a carer to provide care for disabled children. These are duties *if* the local authority are asked to carry out the assessments.

C(S)A 1995 s. 23 (3) & s. 24(1)

5.8

Where a child is 'in need' the local authority have a duty to provide day care for that child during the day if the child is under five or after school and during holidays if the child is attending school (see Chapter 4 for general arrangements about day care).

C(S)A 1995 s. 27

5.9

It must be remembered that these duties relate to the whole local authority and not just to the social work department (see Chapter 1).

C(S)A 1995 s. 93 (1)

6

Orders for children

This chapter briefly outlines the three orders introduced by the Children (Scotland) Act 1995 for the purposes of child protection.

Child Assessment Order (CAO)

6.1

This order was a new introduction to the law of Scotland in the 1995 Act. It allows local authorities (and only local authorities) to apply to the Sheriff to grant an order 'for an assessment of the state of a child's health or development or of the way in which he has been treated'. The Sheriff has to be satisfied that:

- the local authority have 'reasonable cause to suspect' that the child is being treated or neglected so as to be suffering or likely to suffer 'significant harm'; and
- an assessment is necessary in order to find out if there is 'reasonable cause to believe' that there is or has been such treatment of the child; and
- that the assessment will not be carried out unless the order is granted.

(C(S)A 1995 s. 55(1)

6.2

The order can last for a maximum of seven days and must specify the date when it starts and the length of time it is to last. It can authorise the production of the child to anyone for the purposes of assessment. It can allow any type of assessment. One obvious use is for medical assessment, but the order is not restricted to this.

C(S)A 1995 s. 55 (3) & (4)

6.3

There are no regulations regarding these orders, but a child is 'looked after' by the local authority if the order states that the child is to be away from home for the assessment. If the child is 'looked after', the local authority have duties to the child, as listed in Chapter 7.

6.4

There are Rules of Court about applying for such orders. They cannot be obtained on an 'emergency' basis, that is, without giving any notice to a family. They can, however, be obtained on fairly short notice such as three or seven days. If a family wishes to oppose an application for an order, they appear before the Sheriff, who hears both sides of the application.

AS (CC etc.) 1997 Chapter 3 R 3.25 to 3.28

6.5

The Sheriff shall grant a CPO instead of a CAO if he or she thinks that the conditions for it are satisfied.

C(S)A 1995 s. 55 (2)

Child Protection Order (CPO)

6.6

This order replaced the place of safety formerly obtained under section 37 of the Social Work (Scotland) Act 1968. It is not a new remedy, but the new order has different procedures.

C(S)A 1995 ss. 57–60

6.7

Anyone may apply for a CPO and all applications must go to the Sheriff. There are two different tests depending on who is applying. Anyone may apply, but most applications are by local authorities.

6.8

If an application is made by 'any person' (including the local authority), the test is:

- that there are reasonable grounds to believe that a child is being treated or neglected so as to suffer significant harm or will suffer such harm if not removed to and kept in a place of safety, or kept safely where he or she is; and
- an order is necessary to protect the child.

C(S)A 1995 s. 57 (1)

6.9

If an application is made by a local authority, the test is:

- that the local authority have reasonable grounds to suspect that the child is being or will be treated or neglected so as to suffer significant harm; and
- that they are making enquiries to investigate this; and
- that the enquiries are being frustrated because access to the child is unreasonably denied and they need access 'as a matter of urgency'.

C(S)A 1995 s. 57(2)

6.10

The local authority may use either test. Anyone else can only use the test in para 6.8.

6.11

Again, there are Rules of Court about applying for such orders. These orders are dealt with on an emergency basis and notice is not given to the family in advance. Instead, if the Sheriff is satisfied and grants an order the local authority or other applicant must immediately serve or give a copy of the order to the family, as they remove the child. If the Sheriff considers the child is old enough, a copy of the order will also be given to the child, with a special 'child friendly' form.

AS (CC etc.) 1997 Chapter 3, R 3.29 to 3.33

6.12

If a CPO is granted, the child becomes a 'looked after' child (see Chapter 7). Also, the child must be referred immediately to the reporter to the children's panel, who must decide whether he or she will take the case forward to a children's hearing. There are very complicated rules about times within which hearings must be held, and failure to stick to the rules means that the CPO will fall. Decisions about whether the child continues to stay on an order are made by the children's hearing members and/or the Sheriff, depending on whether the family exercises its rights to ask the Sheriff to reconsider the case. Any CPO lasts for a maximum of eight working days at the end of which, if the case is proceeding, grounds for referral must be put and panel members must decide whether the child is to continue to be 'away from home' on a panel warrant (see Chapter 8).

C(S)A 1995 s. 59 & s. 60

Emergency protection

6.13

There are arrangements for Sheriffs to be available for applications to be heard at any time, including out of hours. If, however, a local authority or anyone else are unable to present an application to a Sheriff or anyone else, they may seek emergency protection from a Justice of the Peace.

The Justice of the Peace has to be satisfied on the same terms as the Sheriff, and also that it is not 'practicable in the circumstances' for a Sheriff to deal with the matter. If such emergency protection is obtained, it falls if not implemented within 12 hours. Further, it can last for a maximum of 24 hours, by which time the matter must be put before a Sheriff in terms of a full CPO application, unless the child is to go home.

C(S)A 1995 s. 61

6.14

The police have a similar power to give emergency protection for up to 24 hours.

Exclusion Order (EO)

6.15

Like CAOs, EOs were introduced by the 1995 Act and represent a new remedy. They allow a person to be removed from the family home if the child is at risk, as an alternative to removing the child from home. Only the local authority can apply and the application must be made to a Sheriff.

6.16

The Sheriff must be satisfied that:

- the child has suffered, is suffering or is likely to suffer 'significant harm' because of the behaviour, threats, etc. of 'the named person'; and
- that it is necessary to make an EO against the 'named person' to protect the child, this being a better safeguard for the child than taking him or her away from home; and
- that if the order is made, there will be an 'appropriate person' in the house to care for the child and anyone else there.

C(S)A 1995 s. 76(2)

6.17

Again, there are Rules of Court about these applications. An application for an EO may either be on an 'emergency basis', without notice, or will be dealt with after notice has been given to the family and to the 'named person'.

AS (CC etc.) 1997, Chapter 3 R 3.34 to 3.40

6.18

A Sheriff may grant an EO without giving notice to the named person, but it may be difficult to satisfy a Sheriff that this should be done.

C(S)A 1995 s. 76(4)

6.19

Another practical difficulty is that the local authority, in applying for the order, and the Sheriff, in granting it, have to be satisfied that the 'appropriate person' will fully protect the child and anyone else in the house, and not simply allow the 'named person' into the house 'by the back door'.

6.20

An EO can last for a maximum of six months. When the Sheriff initially grants the order it will probably be as an interim order, whether notice has been given or not. An interim order is as good as a full order, unless it has been granted on an emergency basis. In that case, there must be another hearing within three days, after notice to the 'named person'. Conditions and powers of arrest may be attached to an EO after notice.

C(S)A 1995 s. 79, s. 76 (6) & (4), s. 77 & s. 78 and AS (CC etc.) 1997 R 3.36

6.21

A Sheriff may grant a CPO instead of an EO if satisfied that the conditions for it are met.

C(S)A 1995 s. 76(8)

7

Local authority responsibilities for 'looked after' children

This chapter deals with 'looked after' children, who they are, and what responsibilities local authorities have.

'Looked after' children

7.1

'Looked after' children is the phrase that was introduced by the 1995 Act and replaced references to children 'in care'. It should be noted that the definition of a 'looked after' child is wider than the various definitions of 'in care' and is different from the English definition.

Who are 'looked after' children?

7.2

The definition of a 'looked after' child is in section 17(5) of the 1995 Act. The list is:

- Children accommodated under section 25;
- Children who are subject to a supervision requirement – section 70;
- Children who are the subject of orders, authorisations or warrants issued by the Sheriff or a children's hearing in terms of Chapters 2 and 3 of Part II of the 1995 Act – this includes CPOs and any child away from home on a CAO;
- Children who are the subject of a PRO – section 86; and
- Children who are the subject of orders made when they are transferred to Scotland from other parts of the United Kingdom having been the subject of a care order, etc. – section 33.

C(S)A 1995, s. 17(5), s. 25 & s. 70, Chapters 2 & 3 of Part II, s. 86 & s. 33

7.3

This is a definitive list. If the authority for the placement or keeping of a child is not in this list, the child is not 'looked after'. The list does *not* include children who are accommodated by virtue purely of educational placements, children who have been freed for adoption, or children for whom a refuge is provided in terms of section 38 of the 1995 Act.

Duties of the local authority

7.4

There are a wide variety of duties owed by the local authority to 'looked after' children. These duties are contained in the 1995 Act and the various regulations made thereunder, particularly the Arrangements to Look After Children (Scotland) Regulations 1996.

7.5

The duties listed in the 1995 Act are:
- to safeguard and promote the child's welfare as paramount concern;
- to make such use of services for the children as reasonable parents would do;
- to promote regular personal relations and direct contact between the child and anyone with parental responsibilities, having regard to the child's welfare as paramount and what is practical and appropriate;
- to provide advice and assistance to a child, with a view to preparing him or her for when they are no longer 'looked after';
- to find out and take account of the views of the child, his or her parents and others with responsibilities and rights or an interest in the child, before making any decisions about the child;
- to take account of the child's religious persuasion, racial origin and cultural and linguistic background before making any decisions;
- to carry out a review of each child's case at set intervals; and
- to provide advice, guidance and assistance to any child who was 'looked after' at the date on which he or she could leave school, is no

longer 'looked after' by a local authority and is under 19.

C(S)A 1995, s. 17(1)(a), s. 17(1)(b), s. 17(1)(c), s. 17(2), s. 17(3) & (4), s. 17(4)(c), s. 31(1) & s. 29(1)

7.6

Further details of these and other duties are contained in the 1996 Regulations referred to above. These make some distinctions between children who are 'looked after' and placed (ie. are away from home and placed by the local authority) and children who are simply 'looked after'. The main duties in the Regulations are:

- the details of when the children's cases are to be reviewed;
- the details of care plans for every child who is 'looked after' and the review of these; and
- that a child is medically examined to assess medical needs before or as soon as possible after he or she become 'looked after' *and* placed.

ALA(S)R 1996, regs. 8 & 9, regs. 3–6; reg. 13

7.7

The reviews for 'looked after' and placed children are to be within six weeks of the placement, within three months, and then within every six months thereafter. Children who are merely 'looked after' must have their cases reviewed first of all within three months, and thereafter every six months. Care plan requirements are slightly increased for children who are 'looked after' and placed as opposed to children who are 'looked after'. There is no requirement for a medical examination for a child who is 'looked after' and not placed.

7.8

These Regulations cover other matters such as notification and establishments of records. There are further Regulations governing arrangements for children who are in foster care, children in residential establishments and children in secure accommodation.

Respite care

7.9

This term is not specifically mentioned in the 1995 Act or the Regulations, but the effect of these is that all respite placements which are planned by a local authority and which last for more than 24 hours at a time are treated as 'looked after' placements in terms of section 25 (provision of accommodation, see para 7.10). Such arrangements are therefore regulated and the children are treated as 'looked after' and placed children. There is, however, some modification of the requirements for reviews and medical examinations; only one medical examination is required at the beginning of a series of placements.

ALA(S)R 1996, reg. 17

Provision of accommodation

7.10

The local authority have a duty to accommodate children for whom no one has parental responsibilities, or who are lost or abandoned, or who cannot be cared for by their normal carer, temporarily or permanently, for whatever reason. Such care is often referred to as 'voluntary' care, as it comes about by agreement with parents or carers, or a complete absence of any parent or carer, not because of an order from a court or a hearing. The local authority must provide such accommodation for children up to 18 where they fall into the above categories. Children accommodated in this way are 'looked after' and placed.

C(S)A 1995, s. 25

8

The children's hearing system

This chapter provides some basic information about children's hearings and how they operate, including the involvement of the reporter to the children's panel, the local authority and others.

The system

8.1

The Scottish children's hearing system was introduced by the Social Work (Scotland) Act 1968. It was an innovation of large proportions resulting from the *Kilbrandon Report* and replacing the former juvenile court system. The system deals with children who commit crimes and all other children with social problems. Since its introduction, children charged with a crime are only dealt with in the adult system if the crime is a more serious one (see Chapter 2). Other crimes where children who are charged are under 16 are reported by the police to the reporter.

8.2

The system is not concerned with guilt or innocence but the welfare principle: what is in the child's best interests. This principle is applied whether the child has offended or has been offended against. In other words, one system deals with juvenile criminal justice and children's welfare.

8.3

When the system was first introduced it dealt largely with criminal cases, but over the years more and more cases have been concerned with child protection in its wider sense, as increasing numbers of these have been reported.

8.4

The 1995 Act repealed that part of the 1968 Act dealing with the system, and re-enacted it. There were some changes to and updating of the system, taking account of the lapse of time since the 1968 Act, and also various reports, including the Clyde enquiry into the Orkney case. Nonetheless, the essence of the hearing system as introduced in 1968 remains much the same, including the pre-eminence of the welfare principle.

8.5

Each local authority in Scotland have a panel of specially recruited lay members (a children's panel) appointed by the Secretary of State. The system of panel member selection, training and appointment is maintained by local Children's Panel Advisory Committees, one for each local authority area.

C(S)A 1995, s. 39(1) & (2), Schedule 1

8.6

When a hearing is held it must consist of three panel members, of whom one must be a man and one a woman. One of the panel members with experience and appropriate training acts as the chairman, although he or she has no overriding vote. Decisions are made unanimously or by majority.

C(S)A 1995, s. 39(5)

8.7

The reporter to the children's panel acts in some ways like a clerk to a hearing, but he or she has many other duties throughout the wider system. Since 1 April 1996, the Reporters' Service has operated on a national basis as the Scottish Children's Reporter Administration (SCRA). There is a Principal Reporter and an authority reporter for every local authority area. This system is independent of and separate from the system whereby panel members are appointed.

Local Government etc. (Scotland) Act 1994

Referral to the reporter

8.8

Anyone may provide information or refer a child to the reporter where they think that 'compulsory measures of supervision' may be necessary for the child. The local authority have a duty to refer if they find, after enquiries, that such measures may be necessary. The police also have a duty to refer and any other person may do so. The bulk of referrals come from the local authority, including social work and education departments, the police and health services.

C(S)A 1995, s. 53(1) & (2)

8.9

Anyone making a referral will probably think about the possible grounds of referral (see para 8.14 below) but the decisions about whether there are grounds, and if so, which ones, are for the reporter (see below, Reporter's duties and options). This means that if any person or body is concerned about a child, they can refer whether or not they think there are grounds for referral.

8.10

A child in the hearing system is usually under 16. However, once a child is subject to a supervision requirement, he or she can stay in the system until the age of 18. Any child under 16 may be referred to the reporter, but if it is decided that compulsory measures are necessary, the reporter must be able to have the first hearing before the child's sixteenth birthday, unless he or she is already subject to a supervision requirement. This means, in practice, that the referral of a child to the reporter near his or her sixteenth birthday may be of little assistance to the child if the child is not already subject to supervision.

C(S)A 1995, s. 93(2)(b)

Reporter's duties and options

8.11

When a child has been referred to the reporter, he or she, after 'such . . . investigation . . . as he thinks necessary', has three options. The reporter must:

- decide that a hearing is not required and inform the child's family, etc. of this decision; or
- decide that a hearing is not necessary but that it is appropriate to refer the case to the local authority to provide 'advice, guidance and assistance' for the child in terms of services provided to children 'in need' and other children; or
- decide to arrange a children's hearing because it is felt that 'compulsory measures of supervision are necessary' – in other words, some form of order seems needed.

C(S)A 1995, s. 56(1), (4)(a), (4)(b) & (6)

8.12

Where a reporter has arranged a hearing, he or she must request a report on the child from the local authority, unless one has already been done as part of the initial investigation. Further additional information can also be sought from the local authority which must provide it.

C(S)A 1995 s. 56(7)

8.13

In essence, the reporter's decision to proceed to a hearing is made on the basis that:

- the child needs compulsory measures of supervision, ie. there is a basis for intervention looking at the child's welfare; and

- there is sufficient evidence to establish one or more of the grounds for referral (see below).

Grounds for referral

8.14

A child may be in need of compulsory measures of supervision if any one of the following conditions is satisfied. These are that the child:

a) is beyond the control of any relevant person (parent, carer, etc.);

b) is falling into bad associations or exposed to moral danger;

c) is likely to suffer unnecessarily or have his or her health or development seriously impaired because of a lack of parental care;

d) has had committed against him or her any of the offences in Schedule 1 to the Criminal Procedure (Scotland) Act 1995;

e) is, or is likely to become, a member of the same household as a child against whom a Schedule 1 offence has been committed;

f) is, or is likely to become, a member of the same household as a person who has committed a Schedule 1 offence;

g) is, or is likely to become, a member of the same household as someone against whom incest or related offences in the Criminal Law (Consolidation) (Scotland) Act 1995 were committed by someone else in the same household;

h) has failed to attend school regularly without reasonable excuse;

i) has committed an offence;

j) has misused alcohol or any drug, whether or not a controlled drug in terms of the Misuse of Drugs Act 1971;

k) has misused a volatile substance by deliberately inhaling its vapour;

l) is looked after by the local authority under section 25 (providing accommodation) or section 86 (PRO) and his or her behaviour is such that special measures are necessary for supervision.

C(S)A 1995 s. 52(2)

Hearings

8.15

When a hearing is arranged, whether for new grounds for referral or in continuation or review of an existing case, there are detailed rules about preparation, running and chairing. These are in the Children's Hearings (Scotland) Rules 1996 as well as in the 1995 Act.

8.16

In particular, unless the hearing is an emergency one, the reporter should give seven days' notice of the date, time, place, etc. to children and their families, and, where grounds for referral are put, at least seven days' notice of the actual grounds themselves.

CH(S)R 1996, Rules 6 & 7; Rule 18 (1)

8.17

The child has a right and a duty to attend his or her hearing. If, however, the grounds relate to a Schedule 1 offence, or generally it would not be in the child's interests to attend the hearing, the child may be excused from attendance. However, he or she can insist on attending even if excused.

C(S)A 1995, s. 45(1)&(2)

8.18

In the 1995 Act, the term used for adults with the right to attend a children's hearing is 'relevant person' (not 'parent'). This is anyone, including a parent, who has parental responsibilities and rights, *and* also includes anyone who ordinarily (not by employment) has charge of or control over the child. A relevant person has the right to attend the child's hearing – and a duty as well – unless the hearing is satisfied that it would be unreasonable for him or her to attend.

C(S)A 1995 s. 93(2)(b) & s. 45 (8)

8.19

During a hearing panel members may exclude a 'relevant person' and/or representative for any part of the hearing if they feel it is necessary to do so in order to find out the views of the child or if the presence of the person is causing or is likely to cause 'significant distress' to the child. Where a 'relevant person' is excluded in this way, the chairman of the hearing must explain to him or her when they return 'the substance of what has taken place'.

C(S)A 1995 s. 46

8.20

Before the hearing the 'relevant person' will receive all the reports prepared for the hearing. These are the same reports that are sent to panel members. There is no obligation to give the child a copy of these reports.

CH(S)R 1996 Rule 5(3)

8.21

At the hearing the child and any 'relevant person' may each be accompanied by a representative. The chairman must explain the purpose of the hearing and go over any grounds for referral. He or she must explain the substance of the reports which the panel members and the 'relevant person' have received. After considering the case the panel members must reach a decision. Before the close of the hearing the chairman must tell the child and 'relevant person' what the decision is, the reasons for it and any rights of appeal from the decision. There are also rules about written notification of the decision. The decision could be to continue the hearing (see para 8.26).

CH(S)R 1996 Rules 20 & 21

8.22

Generally, hearings are conducted in terms of the overarching principles, so that panel members must use the welfare of the child as paramount for their decisions, they must seek out and take account of the views of the child, and they must not make an order unless they think it is better to make an order than not to do so.

C(S)A 1995 s. 16

Grounds for referrals and court applications

8.23

Where a hearing has been arranged to put grounds for referral, the chairman must explain the grounds to the child and the 'relevant person'. In order to proceed further, the panel members must be satisfied that the child and 'relevant person':

- understand the grounds and
- accept them wholly or in part.

C(S)A 1995 s. 65(4)

8.24

If the grounds for referral are fully understood and accepted by the child and 'relevant person', the hearing can go ahead. If the grounds are understood and accepted in part, the panel members may discharge the part not accepted and proceed on the basis of that which has been accepted. If the child and/or the 'relevant person' understand but do not accept the grounds for referral at all, or enough to allow the hearing to proceed with an accepted part, the panel members must either:

- direct the reporter to make an application to the Sheriff; or
- discharge the whole referral.

If the child is incapable of understanding or does not understand the grounds for referral, again, the hearing must either direct the reporter to apply to the Sheriff or discharge the grounds, even if the 'relevant person' has accepted them in full.

C(S)A 1995 s. 65(4), (5),(6),(7) & (9)

8.25

If the grounds for referral are sent to the Sheriff, he or she hears evidence on the disputed facts and makes a decision on the normal rules of evidence. The Sheriff either:

- finds the grounds for referral established in full, or in part, and refers them back to the children's hearing; or
- may find them not established and discharge the whole case.

The Sheriff has no power to make any order about the welfare of the child in relation to the grounds. The reporter conducts the proof in front of the Sheriff and the burden of proof falls on the reporter. All grounds must be established on the 'balance of probabilities' (civil standard) except where the child is alleged to have committed a crime, where the standard of proof is 'beyond reasonable doubt' (criminal standard). The Sheriff's decision is not governed by the welfare principle because it is a straight testing of factual evidence.

C(S)A 1995 s. 68

Disposals by hearings

8.26

When there are accepted or established grounds, or there is a review of a case, the hearing has various choices. These are:

- to discharge the grounds for referral on the basis that supervision is not necessary;
- to continue the hearing for further information and/or investigation;
- to make a supervision requirement or continue/vary an existing one;
- to terminate an existing supervision requirement if it is no longer necessary.

C(S)A 1995 s. 69(1), s. 70(1) & s. 73(1)

8.27

A supervision requirement may contain conditions, including where a child lives, what contact a child is to have with others, the ordering of a medical examination or treatment for the child, and a secure condition.

C(S)A 1995 s. 70 & s. 73

Reviews

8.28

It is and always has been an essential part of the children's hearing system that no supervision requirement can last for more than one year without a review. If a supervision requirement is not reviewed within a year it automatically falls.

C(S)A 1995 s. 73(2)

8.29

There are various types of reviews including those asked for by children, 'relevant persons' and the local authority. The main reviews are:
- where the local authority consider a review of the requirement is necessary;
- where the local authority are planning permanent arrangements for the child (PRO or adoption) or adoption is proposed;
- where the child wishes the requirement reviewed (provided it was made or varied more than three months before);
- where the 'relevant person' wishes the requirement reviewed (provided it was made or varied more than three months before); and
- where it is more than nine months since the requirement was last reviewed, in which case the reporter arranges a hearing.

C(S)A 1995 s. 73(4), (5), (6) & (8)

8.30

There is also an automatic review when the reporter puts new grounds for referral to a child who is already subject to a supervision requirement.

C(S)A 1995 65 (3)

8.31

The need for there to be a review when the local authority is planning for permanency means that hearing members must now discuss plans for long-term care and adoption and give their opinion on them.

C(S)A 1995 s. 73(13)

Appeals

8.32

There are rights of appeal within the hearing system, when a final decision has been made or against a warrant. If a final decision has been made by a hearing, the child and/or 'relevant person' may appeal to the Sheriff within three weeks of the decision. The Sheriff dealing with the appeal may:

• uphold the decision; or
• overturn the decision and discharge the supervision requirement; or
• send the case back to the panel members for them to reconsider it; or
• substitute his or her own supervision requirement for the one made by the hearing.

If the appeal is against a warrant, it is heard very quickly and the warrant is either upheld or overturned.

There is a further right of appeal from the Sheriff to the Sheriff Principal or straight to the Court of Session. The reporter has a right to appeal at this stage, as well as the child and/or 'relevant person'. If an appeal is made to the Sheriff Principal, it is possible to appeal again to the Court of Session, with leave.

C(S)A 1995 s. 51

8.33

There is also a right of appeal from the Sheriff when he or she has found grounds for referral established or not established. This appeal is open to the child, 'relevant person', and the reporter, to the Sheriff Principal and/or the Court of Session.

C(S)A 1995 s. 51

Emergency situations and warrants

8.34

Children come before hearings in a variety of emergency situations. For example, the child may be the subject of a CPO, in which case there are strict and complicated time-tables within which the reporter (if a hearing is necessary) must bring the case to the hearing, and the panel members look at the situation. A child may be detained by the police as a result of criminal allegations against him or her, and then be released to the reporter for an emergency hearing. A child may be found by the police where panel members have issued a warrant to find the child, and be brought to an emergency hearing for this reason.

C(S)A s. 59 & s. 60, s. 63 & s. 45

8.35

When hearings meet on an emergency basis they are not usually able to make a final decision. They are, however, allowed to authorise a child's detention for short periods of time, until final arrangements can be made, further investigation can be carried out and/or matters can be taken to court. There is a complicated system of orders and warrants in the 1995 Act, but basically hearing members can issue a number of warrants for up to 22 days each, allowing detention of any child. To issue a warrant, they must be satisfied that it is necessary for the child's welfare or that the child will fail to attend a subsequent hearing if there is no warrant. There is a right of appeal against any warrant. Any appeal lodged must be heard within three days. The Sheriff either upholds the warrant or overturns it, in which case the child returns home. In some circumstances, a Sheriff can also grant warrants.

C(S)A 1995 s. 59 & s. 60, s. 63, s. 45, s. 66 & s. 69, s. 51, s. 67 & s. 68

9

Parental Responsibilities Orders (PROs)

This chapters deals with the way in which local authorities take over the parental responsibilities and rights for a child, taking them away from parents.

Applications for a PRO

9.1

In order to take over parental responsibilities and rights, a local authority must apply to the Sheriff for an order transferring these to them. This procedure is in the 1995 Act and came into force on 1 April 1997. Prior to then, local authorities assumed parental rights through their committees, and this was seen as a confusing process. The new court process is intended to be more open. There are no regulations regarding these applications and information about PROs will be found only in the 1995 Act, the appropriate Rules of Court and the Scottish Office Guidance, Vol. 3.

C(S)A 1995 s. 86–89 & s. 16 & s. 17 & AS (CC etc.) 1997 Chapter 2, Rules 2.37 to 2.44

9.2

Before making a PRO, the Sheriff has to be satisfied that each 'relevant person' either consents to the application or should have his or her consent dispensed with. 'Relevant person' for these purposes is anyone who has parental responsibilities and rights in relation to the child. The court has to be satisfied about all such persons, and it is not now possible for the local authority to take away the parental responsibilities of one parent but not of another.

C(S)A s. 86(2) & (4)

9.3

The grounds for dispensing with consent are that the 'relevant person':
- is not known, cannot be found or is incapable of giving agreement; or
- is withholding agreement unreasonably; or
- has persistently failed without reasonable cause *either* to safeguard and promote the child's health, development and welfare *or*, if the child is not living with him or her, to maintain personal relations and direct contact with the child on a regular basis; or
- has seriously ill-treated the child and re-integration into the same household is unlikely.

C(S)A 1995 s. 86(2)(b)

9.4

These grounds for dispensation are now exactly the same as the grounds for dispensation with consent in adoption (see Chapter 10).

9.5

The Rules of Court for PRO applications are very similar to those in adoption cases. A form is provided for a local authority's application. When the application is lodged, the court appoints a curator (independent person) to prepare a report on the child and his or her circumstances, and a reporting officer to seek out the consent or otherwise of the 'relevant person'. The reports should be lodged within 28 days and thereafter the court will fix a hearing. If the 'relevant person' is not consenting, there will be a proof hearing at which evidence will be led on one or more of the grounds for dispensing with consent.

AS(CC etc.) 1997 Chapter 2 R. 2.38, 2.39, 2.40 & 2.42

9.6

The Sheriff's decisions about PROs (apart from whether there is sufficient evidence to dispense with consent) are governed by the overarching principles: that the welfare of the child is paramount; that the child's views shall be taken into account; and that no order shall be made unless it is better to make an order than not make an order.

C(S)A 1995 s. 16

9.7

In making a PRO, the Sheriff can attach any conditions. These can include contact. There is a presumption that the child will be allowed reasonable contact with the 'relevant person' but it may be necessary to regulate this in the PRO. For instance, it may be necessary to impose a condition that there is no contact or that contact is supervised. Again, this matter is decided with reference to the welfare principle.

C(S)A 1995 s. 86(5) & s. 88

Effects of a PRO

9.8

A PRO deprives the 'relevant person' of all parental responsibilities and rights except the right to agree or disagree to the making of a freeing or adoption order. All other responsibilities and rights are held by the local authority.

C(S)A 1995 s. 86(3)

9.9

However, the 'relevant person' retains the right to apply to court for a variation or discharge of the PRO, although he or she cannot use section 11 of the 1995 Act. Also, there will usually be continuing contact, although this is not a parental right but rather a presumption in favour of the child.

C(S)A 1995 s. 86(5) & s. 88 & s. 11(3) & (4)

9.10

While a child is the subject of a PRO, he or is a 'looked after' child (see Chapter 7).

C(S)A 1995 s. 17(6)(c)

Variation, discharge or termination of a PRO

9.11

Anyone with an interest, including the child, the 'relevant person' and the local authority can apply to the Sheriff for variation or discharge of a PRO. Such an application will not be dealt with unless the applicant can show that there is a reason for it and a change of circumstance.

C(S)A 1995 s. 86(5)

9.12

A PRO can be discharged by the Sheriff. Otherwise, the order will terminate when the child becomes 18 or is adopted or freed, or an order is granted or registered under the Child Abduction and Abduction Act 1985.

C(S)A 1995 s. 86(6)

10

Adoption

This chapter deals briefly with some aspects of the adoption and freeing of children in Scotland.

General information

10.1

Adoption of a child is where a child's birth family is replaced in law by a new adoptive family, cutting off all legal ties and links with the birth family. The child becomes as if born into the adoptive family.

A(S)A 1978 s. 39

10.2

In order for a child to be adopted, anyone with parental responsibilities and rights must either consent to the adoption, or have his or her consent dispensed with. Consent is dealt with in the adoption application or, in some cases, it may be done in an earlier process called freeing. If the child is 12 or over, his or her consent is also required.

A(S)A 1978 s. 16(1) & s. 65, s. 18(1) & s. 12(8) & s. 18(8)

10.3

Adoption and freeing applications are dealt with in the Adoption (Scotland) Act 1978. This Act was amended by the 1995 Act and all references to adoption legislation are to the 1978 Act as amended by the 1995 Act. There are also regulations about adoption agencies and adoption allowances, and Rules of Court.

A(S)A 1978, AA(S)R 1996, AALL(S) R 1996 & AS (CC etc.) 1997 Chapter 2

10.4

Adoption agencies in Scotland are either the local authorities (every local authority must have one) or approved adoption societies (voluntary organisations).

A(S)A 1978 s. 1, s. 3, s. 4, s. 5 & s. 9

Freeing

10.5

An application to free a child can only be made by the local authority. If a local authority is planning adoption for a child, they may choose to deal with consent in the freeing process, before placing with adopters, or to avoid a direct dispute between birth parents and adoptive parents over a child already placed. It is *not*, however, necessary for a child to be freed before he or she is adopted. On the other hand, if a child is freed, there is no question of parental consent in the adoption process, and the court is concerned with the child's welfare only.

A(S)A 1978 s. 18 & s.16(1)

Overarching principles

10.6

The overaching principles and the consideration of religion, race, culture and language (see Chapter 1) apply to 'any decision' made by a court or adoption agency about adoption and/or freeing. This includes all planning decisions by agencies. The child's welfare throughout his or her life is the paramount consideration. Agencies and courts must consider other options and decide on adoption only if it is the best choice for a child. This does *not* mean adoption is a last resort.

A(S)A 1978 s. 6, s. 6A & s. 24(3)

Types of adoption

10.7

The 1978 Act provides for two types of adoption: 'agency' adoptions and 'relative' adoptions. Strictly speaking, no adoption should be arranged by anyone other than an adoption agency, unless it is a 'relative' one. Relatives are defined as grandparents, brothers, sisters, uncles, aunts of the full or half blood, including the father of the child and his relatives if the father was not married to the mother. Most 'relative' adoptions are step-parent ones.

(A(S)A 1978 s. 11 & s. 65

10.8

However, in some circumstances an adoption order may be granted when the child was not placed by an agency *and* is not being adopted by a relative, even if money has been paid. For example, foster carers may seek to adopt a child who was properly placed with them under the fostering regulations, but not as an adoption placement. Or the adoption may be an intercountry one. Courts are allowed to grant adoption orders even where money has been paid.

A(S)A 1978 s. 24(1)

10.9

In practice, most adoptions are either arranged by local authorities or other agencies, or are 'relative' ones, mainly involving step-parents. The legal requirements and processes for both types of adoption are much the same, although some specific issues are different as between the two types.

Who can adopt?

10.10

There is no upper age limit for adoption, although many adoption agencies impose one, but there are lower age limits. Normally people under 21 cannot adopt, but if the adopter is a step-parent, adoption is allowed provided the birth parent is 18, although the step-parent must be over 21. Adopters need to be domiciled in Scotland (ie. consider it as their long-term permanent home, even if they do not currently live there) *or* have been habitually resident in Scotland for more than one year prior to the application.

A(S)A 1978 s. 14 & s. 15

10.11

Adopters are either a married couple or a single person. An unmarried couple (whether heterosexual or homosexual) cannot adopt together; only one of them may adopt, as a single person. In step-parent adoptions, from 1 April 1997 the step-parent alone can adopt if he or she is married to the birth parent who consents to the adoption.

A(S)A 1978 s. 14 & s. 15

Who can be adopted?

10.12

For a child to be adopted, he or she must be under 18 and unmarried. After 1 April 1997, if the adoption petition has been lodged before the child's eighteenth birthday, the application may be dealt with and granted even after the child reaches that age. The child can be of any nationality.

A(S)A 1978 s. 12(5) & s. 65

10.13

A child must have lived with the applicants or one of them before an adoption order can be granted. If the child is being adopted by a step-parent or a relative, or the adoption is an agency one, the child must be at least 19 weeks before an adoption can be granted, and have lived with one or more of the applicants for the previous 13 weeks. This means that an adoption application can be lodged in court for a child under 19 weeks, and who has lived with the applicant for less than 13 weeks, but the petition cannot be granted before then.

A(S)A 1978 s. 13(1)

10.14

Where an application to adopt a child is made by a non-relative, and the child has not been placed for adoption by an agency (eg. foster carer application or a child being adopted from abroad), the child must be at least one year old and have lived for at least a year with the applicants or one of them before the order is made.

A(S)A 1978 s. 13(2)

Pre-court procedures

Non-agency adoptions

10.15

Where applicants wish to adopt a child who has not been placed with them by an adoption agency, they must notify the local authority where they live about their intention to adopt. The notification must be made at least three months before the adoption order is granted. The local authority must prepare and lodge in court a report about the family, the child and all the circumstances of the case. The provisions about 'protected children' (s. 32–s. 37 of the 1978 Act) have been repealed.

A(S)A 1978 s. 22, C(S)A 1995 Schedule 2 para 21

Agency adoptions

10.16

Where a local authority agency wishes to place a child for adoption, with or without a freeing application, there are complicated regulations about procedures and timescales. The adoption agency's crucial stages are the agency adoption panel and the agency decision-maker. No child may be placed by an agency unless their panel has considered the plans for that child and made a recommendation that adoption with or without freeing is the best plan for the child. In every case, disputed or undisputed, the agency then has timescales within which it must make a formal decision and notify this to birth parents and others. If the birth parent indicates within a certain time that he or she is in agreement with the plan for adoption and/or freeing, the agency can go ahead without further timescales. If, however, the parent refuses to agree, or does not return the notification within a set time, the agency is tied by strict timescales. It must lodge a freeing order or ensure that an adoption application is lodged by adoptive parents within very short timescales.

AA(S)R 1996 regs. 11, 12,14,15 & 17

10.17

There are additional requirements on agencies where the child whom they wish to free or have adopted is subject to a supervision requirement. It is now necessary for all children subject to supervision requirements and for whom permanency plans are made to be referred to a hearing for review and consideration of the plans. Where the parent does not agree, and/or the hearing members disagree with the plans, there are detailed timescales which apply.

C(S)A 1995 s. 73(4)(c); & AA(S)R 1996 regs. 13 & 18

Court procedures

10.18

Adoption and freeing cases may be heard in the Court of Session or in the local Sheriff Court. Most cases are heard in the Sheriff Court. The decision about where to apply is made by the person or authority making the application. The procedures for adoptions and freeings are very similar.

10.19

Forms are provided in the Rules of Court for adoption and freeing petitions. They are completed and lodged along with the section 22 report for a non-agency adoption or the agency's own report (section 23) where it is an agency case. The court will then appoint a curator and reporting officer who must report within 28 days. The curator is an independent person providing a view of the case from the perspective of the child's welfare. He or she must also give the child's views, to the court, provided the child wishes to tell them to the curator.

AS(CC etc.) 1997 Chapter 2 Parts II & IV

10.20

The reporting officer is required to obtain the consent of the birth parents, or, if they are not consenting, to confirm that to the court.

AS(CC etc.) 1997 Chapter 2, R. 2.8(1) & R. 2.26(1)

10.21

In Scotland the consent of a child of 12 or over is needed for his or her freeing and/or adoption. The curator seeks this consent, not the reporting officer. The only reason for dispensing with it is because of a child's incapacity.

A(S)A 1978 s. 12(8) & s. 18(8) & AS(CC etc.) 1997 Chapter 2, R. 2.8(2) & R. 2.26(2)

10.22

Where a child has already been freed for adoption, the question of parental consent has been dispensed with. A reporting officer is *not* appointed because no parental consent is required.

AS(CC etc.) 1997 Chapter 2, R. 2.25(2) – there is an error in the Rules here

10.23

After the reports are received, the court will fix a hearing, although it is not obliged to do so in post-freeing adoptions. Where there is a dispute about the adoption or freeing, there will be a proof hearing where evidence will be led. In disputed freeings and adoptions, the court must impose a timetable within which the whole case should be disposed of.

A(S)A 1978 s. 25A & AS(CC etc.) 1997 Chapter 2, R. 2.4, R. 2.11 & R.2.28

10.24

Where the birth parents are not consenting, the court is asked to dispense with their consent. The grounds for this are that the parent:

- Is not known, cannot be found or is incapable of giving agreement; or
- Is withholding agreement unreasonably; or
- Has persistently failed without reasonable cause *either* to safeguard and promote the child's health, development and welfare *or* to maintain personal relations and direct contact with the child if he or she is not living with him or her; or
- Has seriously ill-treated the child who is not likely to be reintegrated into the same household.

A(S)A 1978 s.16(1)(b) & (2)

10.25

As indicated above (Chapter 9) these grounds are now the same as those used in PRO applications. It must be remembered, however, that there are differences between PRO and adoption or freeing processes, and the effects on the child and the birth parents are very different.

10.26

Where parental consent is not given, the court hears evidence in order to decide whether to dispense with it on one of the grounds listed in para

10.24. If the court is satisfied evidentially, it still has to decide on the basis of the welfare and other principles whether to dispense with the consent and whether to grant the freeing or adoption.

10.27

When considering whether to dispense with consent in a freeing application, the court must be satisfied that the child has been or is likely to be placed. A freeing order can be sought for a child who is already placed. A child can be placed while a freeing application is going through court.

A(S)A 1978 s. 18(3)

10.28

Where a court grants a freeing or adoption order and the child is subject to a supervision requirement, the court can terminate this.

A(S)A 1978 s. 12(9) & s. 18(9)

Effects of a freeing order

10.29

If a child is freed for adoption, the local authority take *all* parental responsibilities and rights, and the birth parent has nothing left. The child is *not* a 'looked after' child, but the local authority are expected to provide the same level of service and have the same degree of responsibility as if the child is 'looked after'. Not all 'looked after' duties (eg. maintenance of contact) are appropriate for children who have been freed. Once a child has been freed, the birth parent has no right even to use section 11 of the 1995 Act to seek any further parental responsibilities and rights over the child.

A(S)A 1978 s. 18(5); C(S)A 1995 s. 11(3) & (4)

Effects of an adoption order

10.30

When an adoption order is granted in favour of a couple or an individual, that person or those persons hold all the parental responsibilities and rights over the child as if the child had been born to them. Again, the birth parents, if they have not previously lost all rights through a freeing process, now lose all rights to their child and cannot use section 11 of the 1995 Act to get any further court orders. It is possible to have a contact condition attached to an adoption order, but this is not very common and will normally only happen in 'exceptional' circumstances.

A(S)A 1978 s. 12; C(S)A 1995 s. 11(3) & (4)

Access to birth records

10.31

In Scotland, once an adopted child reaches 16, he or she has a right of access to:

- his or her original birth certificate; and
- his or her court process from the adoption action.

As part of this right of access, counselling services are available but optional. If the adoption was an agency one, the adoption agency which placed the child may also release information from their records, with or without counselling.

A(S)A 1978 s. 45 (5), (6), (6A), (6B) & (7); AA(S)R 1996 reg. 25

10.32

There is no right of access to information for birth families, but counselling is available from local authorities and some voluntary organisations.

A(S)A 1978 s. 1(2)(c)

Glossary

Accommodation
Sections 25 and 26 of the 1995 Act. See 7.10, p.36.

Adoption agency
Every local authority must have an adoption agency. There are also a number of voluntary adoption societies, approved by the Secretary of State, and these are adoption agencies too. See 10.4, p.56.

Agency adoption
An adoption arranged by an adoption agency.

Child
There is a wide variety of definitions of child. See 1.1, p.1.

Child Assessment Order (CAO)
Section 55 of the 1995 Act. See 6.1–6.5, pp.27–28.

Child Protection Order (CPO)
Sections 57–60 of the 1995 Act. See 6.6–6.12, pp.28–30.

Children 'in need'
Sections 22 and 93(4)(a) of the 1995 Act. See 5.2–5.9, pp.24–26.

Contact
This word is used to refer to contact or access between child and parent, child and siblings, etc., whether in the private or public law sector. A contact order, regulating arrangements for contact, is one of the orders listed in section 11 of the 1995 Act. See 3.10–3.18, pp.14–16.

Day care
Care for children during the day, not overnight. See 4.9–4.11, p.21.

Disabled
Section 23(2) of the 1995 Act in relation to children 'in need'.
See 5.6, p.25.

Emergency protection
Section 61 of the 1995 Act. See 6.13 & 6.14, pp.30–31.

Exclusion Order (EO)
Sections 76–80 of the 1995 Act. See 6.15–6.21, pp.31–33.

Freeing
Optional court process by a local authority before an application for adoption, dealing with the consent of a parent to the adoption. See 10.5, p.56.

Hearing
A meeting of the children's panel to discuss a child's case. See Chapter 8.

'In need'
See 'Children in need'.

Interdicts
Court orders prohibiting a person or body from doing something. See 3.19 & 3.20, p.16.

Local authority
Under the 1995 Act, this means the whole local authority. See 1.3, p.1.

'Looked after' children
Section 17 of the 1995 Act. See Chapter 7.

Overarching principles
The three principles listed throughout the 1995 Act. See 1.4–1.7, pp.2–3.

Parent
This means different things in different contexts. See Chapter 3 for the

private law position and Chapter 10 for the adoption one. In PROs and hearing cases, it is a 'relevant person' who has rights, not a parent. See 'Relevant person' (below). Genetic parenthood does not always give parental responsibilities and rights.

Parental responsibilities and parental rights
Sections 1 and 2 of the 1995 Act. See 3.1–3.4, pp.11–12.

Parental Responsibilities Order (PRO)
Sections 86–88 of the 1995 Act. See Chapter 9.

Private fostering
A private arrangement between parents and non relatives. See 4.12–4.18, pp.22–23.

'Relative' adoption
An adoption by a relative of a child. See 10.7, p.57.

'Relevant person'
Sections 93(2)(b) and 86 of the 1995 Act. This expression has two *different* meanings depending on the context:
1. Section 93(2)(b) defines a 'relevant person' for the purposes of the children's hearing system and child protection. See 8.18, p.43.
2. Section 86 defines a relevant person for the purposes of PROs. See 9.2, p.51.

Residence order
Sections 11(2) and 11(12) of the 1995 Act. The effect of a residence order differs in different circumstances. See 3.15–3.17, pp.15–16.

Respite care
See 7.9, p.37.

Step-parent adoption
An adoption of a child by the spouse of his or her birth parent. See 10.7 & 10.11, pp.57–58.

Further reading

McNeill P G B, *Adoption of Children in Scotland*, 3rd edition, Edinburgh: W Green/Sweet & Maxwell, June 1998 (forthcoming).

Norrie K McK, *Children (Scotland) Act 1995 – Annotated version*, Edinburgh: W Green/Sweet & Maxwell, 1995.

Norrie K McK, *Children's Hearings in Scotland*, Edinburgh: W Green/Sweet & Maxwell, 1997.

Scottish Family Law Legislation and *Scottish Social Work Legislation*, Edinburgh: W Green/Sweet & Maxwell, first publication due October 1997; annotated statutes, etc., to be updated regularly.

Scottish Family Law Service, Edinburgh: Butterworths, 1997, updated every six months.

The Scottish Office, *Scotland's Children: The Children (Scotland) Act 1995, Regulations and Guidance*: Vol. 1: 'Support and protection for children and their families'; Vol. 2: 'Children looked after by the local authority'; and Vol. 3: 'Adoption and Parental Responsibilities Orders', Edinburgh: HMSO, 1997.

Thomson J M, *Family Law in Scotland, 3rd edition*, Edinburgh: Butterworths/Law Society of Scotland, 1996.